Level
2

The Nature Kid's Guide to
GOATS

DAVID ANDERSON

LP Media Inc. Publishing
Text copyright © 2026 by LP Media Inc.
All rights reserved.

No part of this book may be reproduced or transmitted in any form or by any means, electronic or mechanical, including photocopying, recording, or by an information storage and retrieval system — except by a reviewer who may quote brief passages in a review to be printed in a magazine or newspaper — without permission in writing from the publisher.

For information address LP Media Inc. Publishing,
30012 Variolite St NW, Princeton MN 55371
www.lpmedia.org

Publication Data

Goats
The Nature Kid's Guide to Goats — First edition.

Summary: "Learn all about Goats, the Nature Kid Way"
— Provided by publisher.

ISBN: 979-8-89818-207-6

[1. Goats – Non-Fiction] I. Title.

Title: The Nature Kid's Guide to Goats

CONTENTS

Goat Goals 4

Mountain Roots 6

Sizing Up 8

Built Tough 10

Super Senses 12

No Ears? 14

Gobbling Goats 16

Goat Gifts 18

Bleat Speak 20

Day Jobs 22

Climb High 24

Goofy Goats 26

Herd Life 28

Stomp and Snort 30

Cute Kids 32

Nanny Care 34

Hard Workers 36

Best Buddies 38

GOAT GOALS

Goats were one of the first animals people ever tamed — over 10,000 years ago!

Baaah! A small goat hops right onto a wooden fence post.

Goats have lived on farms for a very long time. People keep them for milk, meat, and fiber. These useful animals do a little bit of everything.

Farm goats need a safe pen and clean water. They love to run and play in open space. A strong fence keeps them from wandering off — goats are escape artists!

Most goats are friendly and curious. They walk right up to people and want to say hello. Some are small, like the Nigerian Dwarf. These tiny goats stand only about 20 inches tall, making them perfect for small farms.

MOUNTAIN ROOTS

The markhor is the national animal of Pakistan — its name means 'snake eater'!

Clack! A wild goat leaps between the steep rocky cliffs.

Wild goats still live in the mountains of Asia. The markhor is one of the biggest. It has long, twisted horns that curl like a corkscrew — some grow over 5 feet long!

These tough animals live on steep, rocky cliffs. They leap from rock to rock with ease. Snow and cold wind do not slow them down one bit.

All farm goats came from wild goats long ago. People began to keep and raise them. Over many years, the wild goat changed into the friendly farm goat we know today.

SIZING UP
A baby goat weighs only 5 to 9 pounds at birth — about as big as a large house cat!
FUN FACT!
8

Thump! A big white Boer goat jumps off a tall hay bale.

Goats come in a surprising range of sizes. The Boer goat is one of the biggest, weighing up to 300 pounds, heavier than most grown men. These powerful goats have thick white bodies and rich dark brown heads.

Most goats stand about two to three feet tall at the shoulder. Some breeds are barely bigger than a large dog. Others stand nearly as tall as a pony.

No matter the size, all goats share the same bold personality. They run, jump, and climb with confidence. A goat does not know it is small, and it certainly does not act like it!

BUILT TOUGH

10

Scratch! An Alpine goat rubs its head against a fence post.

Alpine goats have strong, sturdy bodies built for hard work. A thick coat of fur keeps them warm in cold weather. Many goats grow a shaggy beard under their chin.

Both male and female goats can grow horns. Some horns are short and straight. Others curve or twist into spirals. Some farmers remove them to keep goats safe around each other.

A goat's legs are short but very powerful. Goats use them to run, jump, and climb steep hills. Their strong bodies help them handle the roughest land.

SUPER SENSES

Swish! A Nubian goat turns its big ears toward a sound.

Goats have amazing senses. Their eyes look different from ours. The dark part in the middle is not round — it is shaped like a flat bar. Strange but useful!

Nubian goats have long, floppy ears that hang down past their chin. Big ears help them hear well. Most goats also have a great sense of smell.

A goat can see almost all around its body without turning its head. It can even spot a fox sneaking up from behind! Those wide eyes keep goats safe from predators.

There are over 300 different breeds of goats. That is more than any other farm animal!

Maaah! A LaMancha goat peeks out. Where are its ears?

Goats come in many breeds. Each breed looks and acts a little different. Some give lots of milk. Others grow long, soft hair for making clothes.

LaMancha goats have very tiny ears. They are so small you might not see them at first! Other breeds have long, floppy ears or short, pointy ones.

Some goats have spots or stripes. Some are solid white, brown, or black. Big or small, spotted or plain, every goat breed is special in its own way.

GOBBLING GOATS
DID YOU KNOW?
People think goats eat tin cans, but they don't. They might eat the paper label off though!
16

Crunch! A goat bites down on a thick, thorny weed.

Goats are not picky eaters. They munch on weeds, bushes, and shrubs. They even eat bark, thorns, and rough leaves that other animals ignore.

A goat has a stomach with four parts. Food goes through each part to get broken down. This special stomach lets goats eat tough plants that cows and horses cannot digest.

Goats like to browse, not graze. That means they pick at bushes and trees more than grass. They use their tough lips to grab leaves right off a branch.

GOAT GIFTS
18

Snip! A farmer shears the soft fur from a fluffy Angora goat.

Goats give people many useful things. Some goats make rich, creamy milk. People turn goat milk into cheese, yogurt, and even soap.

Angora goats grow soft, curly fiber called **mohair**. Farmers shear the mohair off once or twice a year. It is used to make warm, cozy sweaters and scarves that feel like silk.

Goat skin can also be made into soft leather. Even goat droppings are helpful! Farmers spread them on the soil to help plants grow strong.

Around the world, more people drink goat milk than cow milk — over 65% of all milk drinkers!

BLEAT SPEAK

20

Meeeh! A mother goat calls out. She's looking for her baby.

Goats talk to each other with sounds called bleats. A high bleat can mean 'I am here!' A low, deep sound might mean 'Stay back!' Each goat has its own voice.

Baby goats bleat in a soft, squeaky voice. A mother knows her own baby's call. She can pick it out even in a noisy **herd** of dozens.

Nubian goats are one of the loudest breeds. They bleat a lot, and they bleat loudly! Goats communicate in other ways too. They will stamp their feet to send messages and also wag their tails when they are happy.

DAY JOBS

FUN
FACT!
A goat can spend up to eight
hours a day just chewing its cud!

22

Rustle! A goat wakes up and stretches in the morning sun.

Goats start their day early. When the sun rises, they get up and begin to eat. A hungry goat may spend many hours looking for food.

After eating, goats rest and chew their **cud**. What is cud? It is food that comes back up from the stomach. Then the goat chews it again. It sounds gross, but it helps break down tough plants.

As the sun sets, goats head back to their shelter. They like to sleep in a dry, safe spot. A good night's rest gets them ready for another busy day.

CLIMB HIGH

DID YOU KNOW?
Some goats will even climb onto the roofs of houses and barns!

Clatter! A goat scrambles down a steep rocky slope.

Goats are born to climb. Their hooves are split in two and spread apart to grip tight. Soft pads on the bottom work like sticky rubber shoes.

Some goats climb cliffs too steep for any other animal. Wild markhors leap up rocky mountains every day. They make it look easy!

Goats also love to jump. They hop onto logs, boulders, and even fences. A young goat may leap and twist in the air just for fun. Climbing is what goats do best.

GOOFY GOATS

Fainting goats do not really faint — their muscles just freeze for about 10 seconds!

Bonk! Two goats bump heads and then trot off to play.

Goats are playful and full of surprises. They chase each other around the pen. They jump, spin, and kick their back legs high in the air.

Some goats like to headbutt for fun. They back up and — bonk! It is how they play and show who is boss. Even tiny baby goats do this.

Fainting goats are the silliest of all. When scared, their legs go stiff and they tip right over! They are not hurt at all. They pop right back up and keep going!

HERD LIFE

A lonely goat may cry all day and night until it is back with its herd!

Trot, trot! The whole herd moves together across the field.

Goats are social animals. They do not like to be alone. A group of goats is called a herd, and most herds have five to twenty members.

Every herd has a leader. She is usually the oldest, strongest female. The leader picks where the herd eats and sleeps. Everyone follows her.

Goats in a herd look out for each other. If one goat senses danger, it calls out loud. The rest of the herd runs to safety together. There is strength in numbers!

STOMP AND SNORT

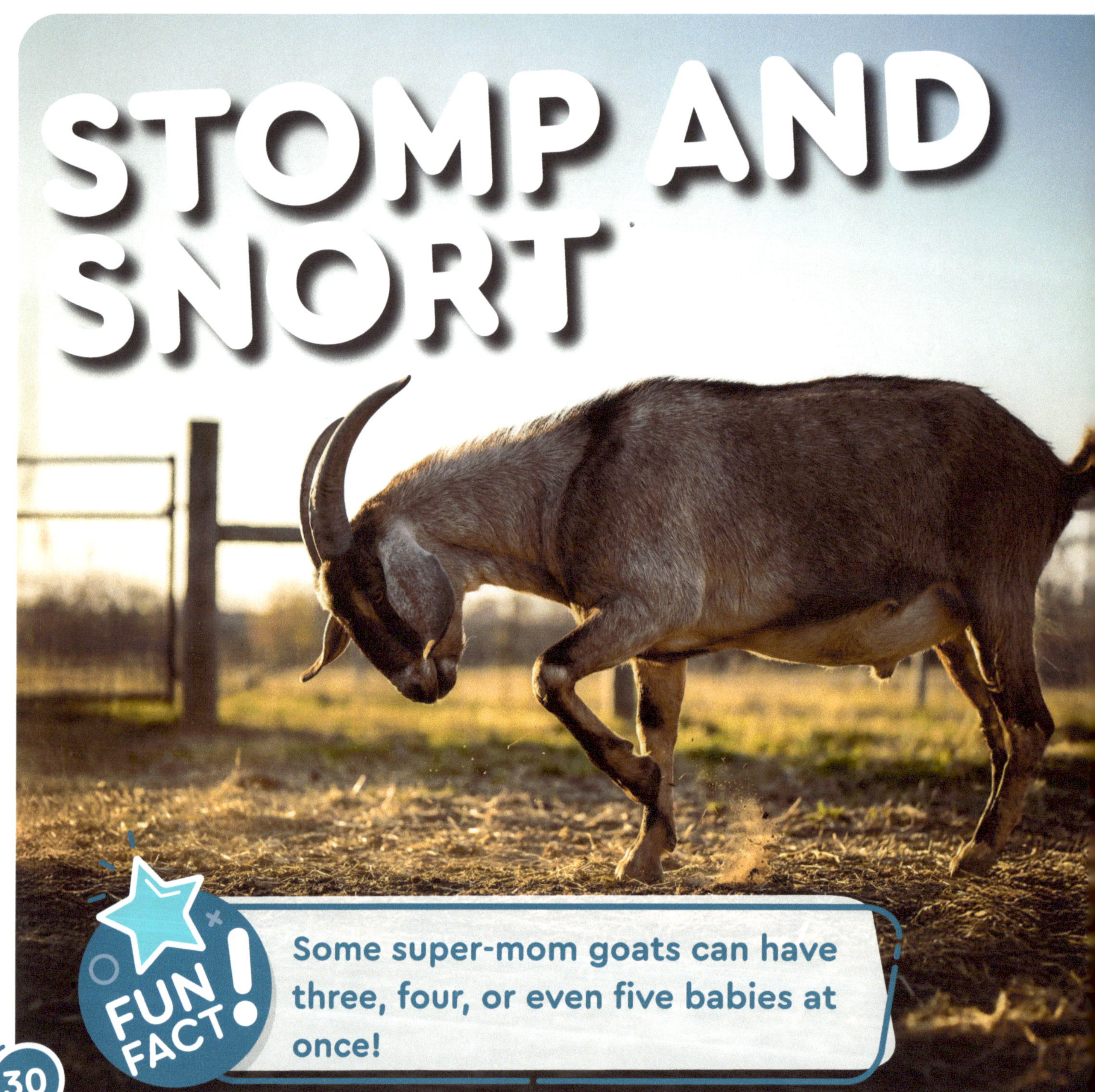

Stomp! A big buck paws the ground during mating season.

Male goats are called **bucks**. Females are called **does**. In the fall, bucks strut and show off to get attention. They stomp, snort, and make loud sounds. The strongest bucks impress the does and get to mate.

After mating a doe carries her babies for about five months. When the time comes, she finds a quiet, safe spot away from the herd. Most does have one or two babies at a time.

The babies arrive tiny and wet. But in less than an hour, they can stand and walk! Soon they are running and playing with the rest of the herd.

CUTE KIDS

DID YOU KNOW?
Baby goats can recognize their mother's voice just one day after birth!

Meh! A newborn kid wiggles its ears and sniffs the fresh air.

Baby goats are called **kids**. They are born with soft fur and wide, curious eyes. A Nigerian Dwarf kid is tiny — it could sit in your lap like a cat!

Kids love to play from day one. They hop, skip, and bounce around the pen like little jumping beans. They play tag with other kids and chase each other in circles.

Young kids drink their mother's milk at first. After a few weeks, they start to nibble on hay and leaves. By two months old, they eat grass and grain just like the big goats.

NANNY CARE

DID YOU KNOW?

A nanny goat can produce up to one gallon of milk every single day — that is 16 glasses!

34

Sniff! A mother goat watches as her kids jump and play.

A mother goat is also called a **nanny**. She takes great care of her kids. Right after birth, she licks them clean from head to toe. This helps them warm up fast.

Mother goats always keep watch. If anything gets too close, the nanny stands up tall. She steps between her kids and the danger. A loud stamp and snort scares most threats away.

The nanny feeds her kids milk for a few months. She stays close and watches them play. A good mother keeps her babies safe, warm, and well-fed.

HARD WORKERS

Chomp! A goat chews through the thick brush in a city park.

Goats help people in many ways. They are great at clearing land. Farmers send goats to eat weeds and brush in places that machines cannot reach.

Some goats carry heavy packs on hiking trails. LaMancha goats are strong and steady, making them great pack animals. They can walk for miles without getting tired.

Goats can even help people feel calm. Some visit schools and hospitals as therapy animals. A gentle goat can bring a smile to anyone's face!

BEST BUDDIES
FUN FACT!
Goats can tell a happy face from a sad one — and they prefer people who smile!
38

Tap, tap! A fluffy goat trots over to greet the farmer at the gate.

Goats make great farm friends. They get along with horses, sheep, and cows. A goat may live with a lonely horse just to help it feel calm and happy.

Goats bond with people too. They can learn their own names and come when called. Some goats nudge their owners gently to say hello or ask for a treat.

A pet goat needs love and space to roam. With kind care, goats become loyal pals. They may even follow you around like a puppy!

GLOSSARY

herd

A group of goats that live together

buck

A male goat

doe

A female goat

mohair

Soft, silky fiber made from the wool of an Angora goat

kid

A baby goat

nanny

A mother goat

cud

Partly digested food that a goat brings back up to chew a second time

www.ingramcontent.com/pod-product-compliance
Lightning Source LLC
Chambersburg PA
CBHW041613110726
48005CB00002B/387